T0160647

The Commandrine and Other Poems

JOYELLE MCSWEENEY

FENCE BOOKS

© 2004 by Joyelle McSweeney

Author Photo: Keeffe McSweeney

Cover Illustration: Florine Stettheimer, *The Cathedrals of Broadway,* 1929.
The Metropolitan Museum of Art, Gift of Ettie Stettheimer, 1953 (53.24.3)
Photograph©1980 The Metropolitan Museum of Art

Published in the United States by   Fence Books
                                       303 East Eighth Street, #B1
                                       New York, NY 10009
                                       www.fencebooks.com

Book design by   Rebecca Wolff

Fence Books are distributed by   University Press of New England
                                       www.upne.com

Fence Books are printed in Canada by   Westcan Printing Group
                                       www.westcanpg.com

Library of Congress Cataloguing in Publication Data
        McSweeney, Joyelle [1976–]
        The Commandrine and Other Poems / Joyelle McSweeney

Library of Congress Control Number: 2004109628

ISBN 0-9740909-3-X

FIRST EDITION

Acknowledgments

The author wishes to thank the following journals for publishing the poems that appear in this book: *Another Chicago Magazine, Born Magazine, The Canary, canwehaveourballback, Colorado Review, Denver Quarterly, Fence, Gulf Coast, La Petite Zine, Los Angeles Review, Monkey Puzzle, Opoponax, Pool,* and *Typo.*

*

"The Commandrine, a Verse Play" received its first performance by the Poets Theater at Open Books: a Poem Emporium, in Seattle, WA, on January 13, 2003.

*

Special thanks to Rebecca Wolff, Eric Roth, Graham Foust, and many others for their input and support during the writing of these poems and assembly of the manuscript, and to Associate Dean Jonathan Michaelsen and the University of Alabama College of Arts and Sciences for supporting the book's completion.

*

Hearty thanks to my friends and colleagues in Tuscaloosa, to my family, and to my husband, Johannes Göransson.

for my mother and father

Table of Contents

The Siren

The Siren

The puppy must be learned of all this material.
No map of the hospital. First, the war effort.
Then, the war itself. The water makes and remakes
its walls. No persons or boats are allowed in them.

This plot is to be played out in the buildings known to us.
Swim for the stick, baby! You've got an anti-sink device.
The NBA guard flips forward and back
in his hologram. Fish-fission. Light.
                              —and found wheels beneath her
linen skirt. The kids mill around like businessmen-clowns.
Their organization is a matter of choice and thus not protected under
reedlight. Candlelight.

Horizonto-rotary gaze beating clearly to the right.
Now, corrected, to the left. Fish! Flip! and Out of Hearing!
Alone in the pink apartment with your little swab.
The moth-mom tries out everything at once: straps on wool,
ties a candle to her head. Don't pity her. She wants to eat the moth!
Which dithers over whether it eats wool or flame.

The skyline lifts, and the gulfstream slips out barefoot
clear to England. Maidens rhinocently down the cowpath clomp.
Toothbrush into yogurt cup, *Recyclamente!* I am so
adamant. The siren with a catch in its cry starts over.
Eternal transistance. Ent'ring our marriage ride.

The Cockatoos Morose

The flowers bend like jockeys
and what a race is had!
A halt up its neck
and its neck against the wire:

finishing wire, graze. and you can keep
as much as you can swallow, doge.

Mine by the white erection,
Mine by the dealership,

et zed.
so said

the Cockatoos Morose

switch off, switchblade, switch-gland operator—
(it switches from what?)

a cool rest for the fingers.
Harmonious—
          (it switches from what?)
Lungwork all around at the gross clinic.
Clutched like the heads of the gods:
grapey, hazard-bearing, *au revoir-dupois.*

(shit keeps falling 'neath the stalls at the state fair)
Kept walking through declaiming
('mid the dark and prize ribbons)
what the brain says in a blackout
(prize!)

under those blacked-out lights

(falling like starlight falls to earth and the earth can hold—

—the Cockatoos Morose

on the eve of privatization, give us a reminder of your regard.
demands that have been excessive or at the wrong time.
a description of its moving ahead.

what disruptive innovation. reversal in the cotalid beds
cycles through the regime. turns out
and around on the civil servant
sipping from the crumpled cup.
because I can do nothing
it's (forgive me) like a dream!

—a cockatoo

Darkness district. how can you unknow?
she only said no once

—the Cockatoos Morose

allow me to benefit from this.
song by the hi and lo waters. bereft of our fragrant mitts!

nil-nil.
           sic, sic.

clawed the foot off. said rump, shake it around.
this is your body and you have to make do.
make it do stuff. reality
on a two-dimensional plane
decorated with
wheels, thistles, celestial wagon-ruts and —eers,
lions (tamed),
a tamer-figurette who covers the lion's eyes

(motherly) with her palm
in an obvious reference—No.
I've got to worry about my own affairs.

she used to watch me more and help me out.

he made himself a cup of instant
and left it to sit in the sink.
sun thickened. stuck drain.

the six guys broke across the house like rain.

—the cockatoos

we rose up our little shade
we were the Canopy Convicts.

the Defunct Cigarette Packaging
Gang. we were the lucky stripe. Green,
we made the ladies wear it.

Falls open in a giving way.

penumbra of this.
disembarkened.
the worn dog wears a bandage
and of course a doggy crutch.
leans at the crook of the boat (admirable! but blinded)

and a row of little bumps rides
shyly in the crook of my thigh.
oh! money is close!

—the Cockatoos Morose

whale throttle: the ligatures
bracing the spines that brace
the studio of my tail and back

the stature; the thrash in my little Seville
about to break
in the falls my lithest craft
about to smash up in the doubling point;

my cocktail my eggcup my equation
lost plus the tickets of their replacement

rotshotgun effectively
rotating air 'til

I was a goddess of history.
genius of peace

(one dream)

Franc sans English our national currency.

everyone said there should be a memory by now and there should be.

tenthousand tons a day for thirtyfive years.

the interior bandwagon. weep among the alien swan.

double-blind, a triple installation.

kill the buddha for existing somewhere else.

it is impossible to order if you're not

in order: you are the boss when the boss is sleeping.

everyone is sleeping. when the boss does

something right—every one will do everything right.

that is the secret of the boss.

you already have it.

that is the conclusion of the boss,

cockatoos.

Application Ballad

I'd been spending my afterlife as a package of frozen *chorizo*
when my sister touched me to her bruised *cabeza*.
I was released and flipped like a djinn
to land with my fin in the sand: *Florida*.
I kept thinking of the blue Barcelonic
sister on the embarcadero,
her feet in sky blue flipflops held on with tiny tongues,
her shelly toetones above the mental water . . .
A wave came in and slapped me over like a pancake.
I was now a puny shark. I fished around for my gills.
I kept my nose towards the bathy shallows
where chance contact might convert me
to a new and useful form. Pale palms and calves dipped low,
bid me closer. I lunged for my benefactress.

Youth Idiom

1.

Inside the sucking melisma,
in the midst of my spring-break-with-the-past,
one of my numerous classmates Melissa
turned to me with sinking hair.

Her visage
firmed up at about the eighth grade. The air
was a converted wet element.
On tensile half-heels we tripped the turnstile,
which rejected my dogeared pass.

Turned back onto streets that cornered into other streets,
along the walls of the flame college,
we traced its exterior for the gate.

Melissa gave me a look that said
Ask any ash tree under the sky
which contemplates combustibility:
rules hold inside this atmosphere
and outside, knocking against each other
from the atomic level on up. To survive,
we bitch out a skinniness;
amid the plentiful univers,
obtain a negative slender.

We still couldn't get inside.

2.

Plus, with wiping,
the corner of my eye produced a seed-size bolus.
Stuffed with pus, it wept uncertainly.

Melissa through my spoiling vision.
We didn't know what to do but sit in the bus shelter,
plexiglas flexing with light.

One bus and then another passed with unresolving
traffic of weird angles, logos,
a world that wouldn't math up. Somewhere the rodeo hopefuls

were tucked into their berths, with their saddles and marvelous
physical lariats, and boot toes uppointing
good thoughts in dark. Hats over their faces

in reverence, in sleep. I wanted to amuse Melissa,
who looked close to abandoning me.
I pressed the heel of my hand
against my zipper, counted teeth.

She grabbed me by the cuff. *Come on.*

3.

In the theater, action blurred like a rumor.
Humphrey Bogart kissed
Bogart, expectantly.

My eye was repeating itself,
splitting the screen and splicing into
other scenes, choosing among times. I became
elevated from the row of seats. Reclining

in the dark air, interfering with the projection,
my own form entered the screen.
Humphrey Bogart and Humphrey Bogart and

Bogart turned to me, and said
Why are you assembling these mirrors?
What do you want to see?

4.

Where was there to go
that wouldn't be a drag? Our money
all run out as images,
we found ourselves back on the street.
Melissa with both hands in her pockets,
her elbows pointing backwards, lowslung,

produced a gust which steered us to the travel agency.
A wash of blue stood for the Caribbean.
Melissa read the fares *we could go* and *we could go*

She had so much to say it was a world of talking!
It was uncharacteristic and a delight.
I let my eyes blur out till I could see the pins and needles
plates and barbells, rods, the shape of vision

without content. My face felt cold and hot. I felt anything
I could turn to I could understand. But my eye
corrected me. *Don't you know*
the riddle? I am that world I cannot see.

5.

A baby without bones looked up at me
from the puddle of itself at my sneakersole.

It was as far away as Florida and as I looked at it
its boneless body shifted into coastline
and panhandle.

By instinct I sucked a big breath and sunk
into the watery part of the map. So this was the gulfstream,
relatively warm,
carrying the coconuts across the x-wide Atlantic
to British coasts.
There the ocean was rendered
as a field of flexing arrows
which lowered onto me, a *mandolina*. I was severed into various parts

We floated together at the same rate
away from America.

6.

In the morning, my cheek could not lift itself
from roughness. My wrists and my ankles
persuaded me to reassemble.

I turned over and looked up. Her back to me,
I recognized Melissa by her parka.

Her legs curled away from me on the bench.
Paths of corduroy, sneaker treads.
I contemplated these, and realized my vision

was minute again. I got to my feet.
It was a small city park and I could see its edges.

I followed the footpath
out and down to the river
rushing in the morning like thousands of quarters

from the slot of the west, where the sun was heading.
Above me, the sky was a bowl to catch them
could it only be slid.

I studied the problem.

Click Track

Vision makes the first line.
Celeriac. Valerian. Climbs
into fiber. A xylic fitness, worn for years
to cinch bedclothed waists into piety.

If you freeze each frame, you can see it vegetate—
frill and bloom, then clink into calcification.
Limited man, delimiting. Somewhere, a shelf crumbles.
From the tightness with which this fits,
you may infer full proof.

Click, click. The debt orchestra taps its stands
from somewhere overtheradio. It is so clear
even volume doesn't make it clearer. Leant effort.
They're swept clockwise in the tide
like a single white medallion keep
crossing the meridian-line: o'clock, o'clock.
Click track. Caprice in the fake foyer.
There the bulb blossoms from sharp tin painted little leaves
profligating from chains. It is likened to a coppice gate
in Shangri-La, the chandelier's interior, integuments,
girths, silhouettes, earth's links
and gravities, earth's rules, earth's earthly etiquette.

To confront the sorrow. To spare this station
from chaos and abnegation and doom. To spare this sparrow
who picks at the tieline

holding up the suet
though not at the suet:
the blue plastic integument.

Inspector of schools, overzealous.
Overlooking the azalea blooms,
we were only record players, racquet bearers.
became a cliffhanger,
became a phalanx-de-troops, stood on the cliff,
lookdover, wind ruffling the mutated frill
that stretched from our necks like a hood—

Practical as an electron, it exists
in a state of murky possibility, buying
things for dinner, looking for signs
of dinner the next day. It worked till it crawled
into its substratum, pupils slotted sideways
like a goat's. Uncertainty planet.
What's the view from here. To be anywhere at once
is to be nowhere. I remember warm tides;
I must be misremembering. The universe and its laws
must have come in from somewhere. Number
pinned to its shirt. How long can this series continue
and simulate care for its results.

The policy kept retightening,
retendoning, the tent thick with integument, musclebound.
The video looped
through its three tongues:
parvenu, bien venue, a huge
and generous site. The skate-announcer tossed
his mantle of tissue. It flopped slimily

over his eyes. V. rode in on the third epicycle,
the lining shuddered from its heights.
Shed, revealed new lining.

Blue Suet

1.

Minarets in the groundweed, a camel pack. The drainpipe-cum-eave
extends a blue cage from which meat has escaped as birds.
If the line is drawn out far enough,

the birds are still here. ex libris. out of freedom,
into freedom. Leads the camel train.
Digs up boxes and examines their contents. Desert tilting like the face

of the desert reassembled as a tomb. Moon
alters, tomb sinks. The burrowing asp
digs a whole to another climate.

2.

On the grate is the world's number one extreme eater.
Passes over the bound blueflies, pulls the whole web with him
as he scales for leafmeal. The knight's grill

falls into place. If the greaves
cartoon *a weight settling,* our
fantastically jointed companion

demonstrates the space which contains
all inner motion and of all outer motion
marks the limit. wears our ribbon.

Bureau of

This is the body of,
waiting to turn on.

graced with a little tremor,
a little-known form, a fibrous hook,
a flimsy lever that makes the jar work

a lever and a clasp

:*voila*. The pathetic filofax
unfurls, the owl describes;
on air; makes an apse; lopes left

off the phonepole, woodenly.
we rise above the wind park,
commemorially.

our whorled fossil, pinned open.
our emergency kit
holds aspirin. digitalis. adrenalin-in-in.

Lives

1. It was the handgliders, soaring o'er the rusty field. Drone of the mower, drawn. The afternoon absolutely faunless. As under the glassy dome, the long-tailed bird is prostrate, dry hillside degrades. Tangle of broken limbs. Attention inverts the curve, closes in. *It's a baby! I think it must be the little girl from T.V.!*

2.—the thought stays cosseted. The pencil skirts demand the trays be lifted at a stiff and difficult angle. A sort of swivel devotion. The sacred compound slips from its mold, the mind in its perfect botanics shifts air and heat through its convections. How it functions. How it makes the legal tender.

People mill as through the universe through the loft. These are the survival particles, sifted through the first Great Bend, assembled in the studio kitchen for demonstration of the Miracle Blade System. Smocks and toques. The paring knife, for example. How it fillets the fillet.

3. Names for the gods who promoted fertility and protected sailors. Now *that* was a flame who could leap! The fiber pounded soft with a pestle, pounded forcefully, the flower of the army turning its face southerly, southwesterly like a dayclock. On the vulnerable shore, turning its facet. Its singular, bright sword.

Vulnerable, but rocky. The counters gleam to the touch but are lightless, moon-lustre being totally absorbed as cold. Here the troops have been billeted. In hearing-range, neptunal variations.

Cassette! A small past betrayed into presentness. Rewound, comes wrenching from the teeth. *There are two kinds of beans here and they both stand for the soul. Les beans mignonettes. Little girls, little girls. I had a dream about a dive in the afternoon; I didn't go there. Manchester-by-the-sea, I'm local. I live here but I never see the ocean.*

4. Neptunal variegation: Understand that inconsistencies are the point of the fabric and part of its natural beauty. Not to mention its costliness. Can you understand? A nominal cost—what would that be? A spark, some spit, a speck of dust? The money hangs around with its faces to tell us something. We add it and we use it to get clean.

5. We divide it: wick & cloth. Although there is a temptation to set the numbers going backwards, resist it. Nothing works that way. There have been rumors that without witnesses, there is no event but it doesn't hold. Nothing can hold it. The present tense. I'm as sure of that as of standing here.

6. Our wrists work in sowing motions as we toss out our little nets. We're dreaming of a trip to the mainland where we can walk on grass. You could tie a skirt to the mast, support it. This could work by darts. A card with buttons and a card with rick-rack—

7. Enough felinity! The mash in the bowl is just that. Part salt-petre, part corncobs and part burnt crabs. Their brains are transferred to the smoke that rises, a daemonic being. It will do our bidding, depending on what we bid. What price. What fine pairing. Undo the cord and dump the leaves out on the rock. How they clump prefigures what we'll pay for next.

8. Air went wrongways down the oxygen mask. It wasn't long till he
was crushed like a cab. And long limbs disappearing all the time.
Let's not forget how this got started: The costs were exponential, then
the corners were cut. Without corners, everything rolled just fine
until the flatland. Then we stuck.

We reached for our handcarts but our hands were gone. It'd been in
the contract all along but finely printed. The finest print was so
difficult to read, always spiraling off into nonsense erudition. Gilt
and red dye rubbing off in our——

Two sides of the same coin, I say. But if we had two now we'd have
two to rub together and with a little tinder we'd have flame.

Which brings us back to legal tender. Which brings us back to the
body consumed, divorced, was found, was over, but something was
made lasting in the mind which rips and snags around it, so that the
flow is distorted, the current siphoned off to power the vanity
generators of the boomtowns along the plain. To provide water unto
roofs now guttering into night: of Baseline and Showlow

The Commandrine, A Verse Play

Scene 1: *Bunks: The sea like a bedsheet. The Sleepers Awake!*

SAILOR 1:
Why dream of a lion
mane brilliant ribbons

in the chest that spins
like a derrick.

off the highdive

lion off the highdive into earth
spinning disemboweling the earth

SAILOR 2:
left here
is the stranger structure
hear in the chambers—large with pith
or succulent small and with a finer
acidic stitch ah. I am   like a girl
glamorously entrapped
in my lemon house
in my house made of lemon.

SAILOR 3:
silence!
silence!
silence!
silence

is almost always an overstatement!

SAILOR 4:
Those guys are bad liars,

racing, rise like kite wires,

brighter and littler
          sun burnt bad
liars to squint.
squint long after 'em
blind you too. my blind
-spot brother. sun-spot liar!

Scene 2: *The Commandrine. A.M. Lullaby.*

COMMANDRINE: like anything that grows cell by cell
we worked out the first vague plan of ourself
people, people.

gilled and web fingers girled with light
our eyes were spots for sensing light
people.

now the four boys trail on the sea
like pinstripes to our mind

like contrails like excrescence.

boys. shall we urge you home?
your teachers and students gather in halls
and wings, the chambers

sealed against summer
through windows through doors wrenched open

fill with heat!

Scene 3: *The Boys. Systems Go. The Devil*

s4: Auxiliary Air Systems—check!

s1, 2, 3: Swim bladder, coke cans, pockets of caves, backseat of a car
tipped sinking, spare tires; bubbles in bread; flutes and needles;
shunts; collapsible/inflatable cup; broken seal; pay envelope; ear
canals. what slips from the neck intó the bottle when the bottle
pours; compressed in what pours. what rises when the contents
settle.

s4: Right. and the prize.

s1, 2, 3 (to S4, in admiration): Sir!

DEVIL: (in white suit, with mixing bowl) Gentlemen, kitchen light, the
curtain lifting,what fills a coolness, the hand that sleeps and knows
its way from spoon to bowl, bowl to mouth, gentlemen! this
sweetness that sugars the grain is hardly tasteable, do you not own it,
is it not your birthright, and given to you and waits in a dry place?

s4: Sir. How come you to our ship?

DEVIL: I visit all ships. For the education of men.

s1, 2: For our edification!

DEVIL: For that purpose.

s4: I am suspicious. Men, interrogate.

s1: How do you get your suits so white?

DEVIL: Gentlemen, I object.

s4: Answer!

DEVIL: Gentlemen, I subject them.

s2: To what?

DEVIL: Dry heat. And my teeth to paste. And my socks, to soap and high water. coast, zest, irish, ivory—

s3: He knows our names!

s4: Sir, how do you know our names?

DEVIL: I've come for you.

s4: For what?

DEVIL: To fetch you home (waves hand; small explosion).

s1, 2, 3, 4: (all groan with disgust)

s4: (to DEVIL) Firstly, your melodrama is distasteful and a bad example. You call yourself an educator!

s1, 2, 3: (rooting) Sir!

s4: Secondly, ours are but routine maneuvers and hardly justify this sort of homemongering.

s1, 2, 3: (to DEVIL) Fie!

s4: Finally, we are inoculate. In that our ship is well supplied. Soap, foodstuffs, toothpaste, tables. Racked chest-high.

s1, 2, 3: Gah!

s4: Ready the vessel, men. We're putting this man ashore (exits)

DEVIL: Delightful! (gathering his belongings) Gentlemen, your officer here has issued his decision. I shall not trouble you again.

(the entire ship/stage rises off the ground and hovers one third of the visual space down from the rafters. the floor of the theater spreads so that each seat is at the center of a circle about six feet in dynameter. At a variety of slow-to-alarming paces, each chair pivots with its audience member. the chairs sink and rise into the theater floor slowly, but, importantly, at no time does any audience member sink below chest level into the floor. let this continue for 1.5 minutes. then ship/stage lowers down into its original position. COMMANDRINE)

Scene 4: *Commandrine*

COMMANDRINE: People, reports have been alarming.
And I admit that was peculiar!
Are you not in your seats again and facing forward?

Just off our waters,
Zest, Coast, Ivory and Irish raised their hump
and poked a White Man through their blow hole.
He was immediately lost in the spray.

I think we all know who that was.
the Homunculus!
Climbing away. Then our four men disengaged
from our harbor, submerged their submersible.

People,
What does it mean that they continue their routine
down there, without a sprite, without a soul?
I'll think you agree that this is urgent.
that I must urge them home.

Zest! Coast! Ivory! Irish! Shall I urge you home?
There is a placemat and a wiped-clean table
and a mug and a bowl . . .

What is a fact? both hook and sinker, it snags
but doesn't change
except as it breaks
its fabric, its predicament.

the lesser lights, in accordance with
the Big Fact, bend like a cord
of sea plants in the current
when the sea begins to breathe

32

fact into circumstance.
Shall I excise them?
Shall I exercise my command?

Scene 5: *Shipboard. The Happy Men.*

s4: Knots!

s1: Overhead, figureeight, slip, loop, bowline—

s2: square, spit, granny, correct, carrick-bend—

s3: hitch clove hitch half hitch bend

s1, 2, 3: Matthew Walker!

s1: Interlacing!

s2: twining

s3: looping

s1, 2, 3: Or the like!
          binding or connecting two cords together . . .
          or a cord to something else.

s4: Good. a group or cluster of persons or things.
     folded upon itself.
     the crossgrained
     mass of wood
     where a branch joins a tree (frowning)

s1: a protuberance. an excrescence, the inside made
     inextricable, inextrinsic, inextractable. fungal and bile!
     roiling—

s2: —how in a pot the bubbles roil
     and KNOT! a swollen form, a problem,
     intricate, involved, face burnt from watching steam

s3: Naut! A unit of speed
      one nautical mile
      per hour sinking and standing
      up and measured against a bubble level

s1, 2, 3, 4: one point fifteen statute miles o
             when will they tie—the knot! O
             Commandrine—when will they marry? interpolate.
             one of the points at which values are assigned
             in a function (big breath)

TO SECURE OR FASTEN BY (breath)
TO FORM PROTUBERANCES, BOSSES OR KNOBS
TO BE ENTANGLED IN A (breath)
TO MAKE (breath)S!

s3: (sweetly; a ditty)
        when in the knot garden
        my truelove said to me . . .
        the gridding of the branches
        the sieving of the breeze
        the involuted feeling of the fast-inspiring sea
        drew all its inhalescence down to me! down to me!
        focused all its inhalation into me!

Scene 6: *a half scene. the Devil carrying wood. he sings, fashions a table.*

DEVIL: My apothecary is always needed.
          my periodic and my stable
          system of table legs. four.
          or three, well-placed, will do.
          at any rate more than two.

          this steady square ziggurat!
          or this library of tiny slots, doors,
          cabinets. or the door of shade
          yawning deeply under any structure.

          some think they are equal to
          one thing, their nemesis.
          to look out for.

          'here is a carbon ring
          and tab oh to slot oh-two, children,
          beware my pretty trap!'—not so.
          it's garbage. let them think they have seen through you

          that the pact is broken, o,
          then it's the first thing they settle on!

          (spreads a checkered cloth)

          gentlemen. lunch!

Scene 7: *The Boys—the Men!— at table. Empty platter. Postprandial chat. All round the chamber pieces of a white suit hang neatly.*

s3: The Duke of Wellington—

s2: There were five dancers—

s3: He raiséd his cockade hat—

s1: His coq-au-vin!

s2: And they turned this way and that—
　　　　pantilines bending the pictureplane

s3: Up the hill, down the hill, his charger,
　　　　his magnificient change-up.

s1: And then the Russians came right through the glass—

s2: and yelled

s1, 2, 3: Bistro!

s3: and that's where the term comes from.

(each pounds the table thoughtfully and stands. s1 grabs the platter and hands it to s2, then sweeps up the table cloth and hangs it as a curtain. s3 breaks down the table, making a neat stack of wood to the rear; s2 drags out a cardboard box of gleaming platters arranged with their rims peeking out and adds his platter to the series. The stage set may resemble the interior of a log cabin. It's still a ship, though.)

s4: (entering w/sonorous dignity) Men,

s1, 2, 3: Sir!

s4: sonorously, men, I have considered it.
drowsing over my charts.
in my close cabin consumed.

s1, 2, 3: Lunched!

s4: Well more 'absorbed' in the sense of 'thoughtful' . . .
also, it's more of a bunk (dreamily) where I drew
from the bank of knowledge . . .
let's discuss possible routes.

s1: Sir: Gulf States: this term compresses two geographies; being
Florida, Alabama, Mississippi, Qatar, Louisiana, Iraq, Texas/Bahrain,
Kuwait, Oman, Saudi Arabia

s2: and the U.A.E. By way of comparison or else associatively.

s3: or else through the construction of a pump. an assemblage.
sodium, sump—

s1: a charge carried through the water, our craft rubberized, so that
we rode atop current—

s2: not rowed. too dangerous—

s1: not rowed, perhaps lifted by the thrust of it—

s3: the gist of it—

s1, 2, 3: Yes!

s2: and careful not to list,

s1: providing the rubber is thick

s4: enough.

s1, 2, 3: Sir!

s4: Thick enough to resist. This plan needs work. Let's consider it auxiliary. (gesturing to the suit) and how is our immaculate friend?

s1: Difficult to digest.

s2: hard on the maxillary.

s3: tough. A hard nut to crack.

s4: cracked nonetheless.

s1, 2, 3: (admiringly) Sir!

s4: (twinkling) Bunks; dream on it. (SAILORS exit.)
(alone, eyeing suit)
(exits!)

Scene 8: *The Commandrine. Midnight.*

COMMANDRINE: Boys, the people are asleep.
Fishing nets, widow-weeds.
darning socks and damning
rivers!

lochs and sleives, locks and sleeves,
people, boys, and the dinner coals
which are now softly
embers.

softly stoically stow home!
on your own craft, make way.
all the feathers in the bolsters
would flap for you

if they could. and all the bread would mold.
and the soft lamps of home
crack and conflagrate
the ladders

lofts, cribs and trundles
in which your people sleep.
and on that rising ashen current
your could sail your boat

boys in your bunks
pallet-boys

come home.

Scene ?: *The Commandrine. Thoughtful. With book, notes, compass, chalkboard.*

COMMANDRINE: 'Swing gait go down in the stumble!
the rider in fall finds four feet.'
how does that work—to sink with your scene
intact into the chamber of the present.

'the past is a fulcrum—a filament
burning the hand of he
who would follow—' a diaphragmatic action.
(stands)
ways of committing enduring knowledge:

snap and receive, huddle toothdown
among the players—torque at the nape—
Independent. hand
wide as a catcher's mitt, mapping this visitation

(*x*es on chalkboard)
here— and here— and here—
this should be shapely. the plastic idea
and the head of the rood—

(one *x*)
there. isn't that a part of culture? humiliation?
grow up fat push together and fall in your season.
as we will subsequently celebrate.
the pinched head for getting in holes.

at dawn, the trees piece the lawn together
a pool of an instant—'now this is armed and ready to be used'—
pressurized shotgun and carbon diox shells
propped against the porthole, ready. (sits. stands.) of course

the shark can't breathe, his stomach blown
through his gills. dirt blows
in the bunker windows and collects on the sills.
at one point five million dollars saved

in travel time per taxpayer down
since the ten percent increase in speed. . . .

the grand scheme is out.
the dome and all that.

FIN

Joan

Joan

Crusade-dream flips like a standard. The standard
narrows to a point. And points.
Then it dips like a fern.

In the *bois chesnu,* little rotted shells
crunch open. Lit in dark,
the fibers underground hiss *I'm optimisstic.*

Carry this information: When an ant dies,
it's going to tell everyone. Astream,
the loverbeetles scuttle the lilyhouses, while,

up on the moonline, the fat sub rises
in a lather, clutching his leaflets. He
has a crazed look in his eyes. *Hee*

hee lee lion luh lion I
would take a pride an hour
to consume (the buttons rotate in his coat).

On that bed of grass and guts what's brought
to close and open history? You experts dressed
as bucket-hatted clowns:

I don't want to learn today.
Snow her into the conifer.
We have a troupe of fall guys

and I have never liked her.
Bebop vet'ran over the bebop ruins, chop.
I have built this mechanism. Jumped into its arms.

What I Eat is a Prayer

Then in the August of my twenty-seventh year,
naked except for my seaclogs,
I greeted an audience of piers.

After my dip, I came up covered
in salt and sand: hair tough as an angel's.
Who could disappoint me now among the so-coifed?

Disappointing menus for a banquet of twenty-seven.
The hostess cannot hear the hotelier, walls blow ope';
lousy with wallets and checkbooks, the air. Naked except for

The checks and the monies flapped like birds.
I partook of the seasonal activity
and caught a check in my hands—to myself from myself—

and was caught; I was smart and dumb.
I hadn't been clobbered in such a long time!
Now, shoved against the carpeted headrest,

I wondered at its cold and slender neck.

The nakeder I feel the happier.

Camp is over, and the children come out
wearing hats; the children are happy for each other,
each camp having been maximally appropriate.

The ocean grew gritty with proteins. I arose
and clomb to the yard with its spigot.
It looked up and blinked. Above, kite strings wrote

toing and froing was the same motion; tiny sighs above the halls
at the county airport; swung on tiny chains;
my father swathed me in two handtowels,

said *nexttime, swim in the sea.*

A gold thread falls from an eagle's towel
onto the beach. A gold face big as a quarter of the sky
looks at us with gold-milk tears in its eyes

and the gold girl goes on brushing the countryside
with a twig-broom big as a tree. When our competitor
finishes third, he approaches the throne

with a gold wheel of tillamook.

Bugs Bunny, Or, The Mirror That Hid a Little Camera

I'm rundown.
I have a sunburn.
These ears are my liability but they hold a lot.

Like the crazy wheel on the shopping cart,
I schlep and schlep.
Then I pour out all my opera like an anvil.

Battle Scene

In the foreground, the general's
topcoat. The inside apple-white.

Most suffocate in the collapsing tunnels.

In the background, I've already deserted.
I skate around the millpond
with wooden blocks for feet.

When I notice the locals catching on,
I become a little strut in the bridge.

Demos

We wheeled the volcano from state to state.
From the ash we fashioned vistas.

We relished effluvia. At those extremes,
we lived without differentials.
Ourselves, others. We salvaged the heatseekers
and cast off the weaponry. Bacteria
swept the ocean like decimals, barcoding the currents.

The reef disbanded and was reassembled
in the bays of a converted bomber. Launched
into the paunch of the storm, our meters
not only monitored but analyzed it.
The black clouds were deseeded and reined in.

At the hangar, there was a curling
in the pages of the manual, an inner
complication, an ever-paisling structure
making inroads in the pods. With the tips
of our toes we could almost
taste it, we could almost put our finger on it

The Wind Domes

Everyone knows that time unfolds
as events into the particular. His shredded shirt

floats down as cloud ripples. These are his motion-
and his power-lines

receding through the valley.

His shoulders one shade greener than the sky.
The valley two shades greener.

go back after—songs waft from the box
encouraging us to go through with it.

To be a worthy continuum.
To be a moral compendium
in the dark green chickpea glade—

       I'm a kid so I can't   go anywhere.
       You'll have to   bring it to me.

—in the frosted flakes of grain
in the rushes where, if you pull one up,
they scream or interrogate you.

Emptied of their po-et-ree
they lie in the potters' field.

The vessels, I mean. The protest of the dog
in the throat of the evening
makes the evening suddenly deep.

The Problem of Knowledge is
what to do with it,
            once you have it.
(Sign this form.)
(Paste a picture of your skiff, here)

            gamboling debt
on the rambling see.
The little deck shifting
like a slopéd glen (Paste
your thumb to it. Thumb*print,* you clod!)

a-clearing. The buck's rack glinting in retreat.

I lift it like a flashcard and it gathers no _____.
Lift it like a fish from life.

and how am I to convince you, if you aren't here to convince?
Those people just aren't here anymore.
They split. They left the club. I told you
(I woulda told you) like a bathmat or a bathroom's drudge
-light to make do with. To make
right by. There is no second life.

Plutonium wristlet appears as a circle of fireflies
as she crosses the humpéd lawn.
The closer they get,
you can see the holes between them.

Slipped from her wrist, plunged to toss in the bed
that ran from the summer capitol.
The river, I mean. Sunk down
to surface again
in the cluster. Magnified.

How it gave off a summery light.

The Air Sign

In the river of luggage and pieces of the bridge,
I felt a scaly muscle rise between my thighs
and that was the joy side.

Rode it to safety, but safety
did not treat me well this time. In decline,
I besieged the Creator
with harp-cries, with the tenacity
of the already gone. The truly gone.

The joy side: How to keep it with us. Direct address to the hero
in the gallery, continual engagement, 'a head from behind
kept pushing me up,' refused the lifeline,
gestured to the circuit of victims.
The nylon ladder
beneath the helicopter
traced a disheveled wreath
but could not grapple.

this view
is looking out at the famous plant
in the Oregon countryside; cheese is produced here
and Highway 101 is on the right, where you can't see it.
Outside the limits of the cheesecam. Your sweet

imagining
cannot be truncated.
Piquant and tongue-chastening.

Innitiation

Strolling on the petite meadow of your ass,
below a bloom of 'hot' machinery,
we bit open pellets to retrieve the red magnesium
which rose up to the factory ceiling,
where it caught on the heat beds and exploded.

Up on the rooftops for a false spring
also lit by explosive elements stuffed in foils.
That was the bar called 'flowers,' and you knew why'
as we turned our hot faces to the lamp. With stiff, fixed fingers
we couldn't undo our dour zippers.

They kept sticking in 'off' position. Goddamn!
they jammed their own works. The heavy-bottoms
dragged the channel and couldn't exist.

Let's say there was a blackboard beside the field day.
I caught a hurdle and went careening.
then an older girl taught me the principle of multiplication.
These days I'm archemedic—how much is displaced
by this heavy way I trough the day-bin.
A lesson on poetry from which an algebra lesson
begins like a chicken. Learn, and leap.

Spectacular Attacks

When you hear of spectacular attacks,
recall how they will appear in night vision—
green, blooming into the sky,
tight-sprawling Easter sprays.
This is the heat the building yields:

a familiar production. When the bear pedals short,
the cloth clown climbs a wire
to defuse what's perched
atop the telephone pole.
This is the confusion of a volatile formula,

the outflowering of nourishment
bad and good for you both. You clutch
at what flies from you. You watch
from the outside, wandering brick.

The Born Fetus

The born fetus is a born scientist.
Flips his dish. Tries to glean a tan
from the overheads. Among the corrugated
cardboard and six-ringed empties,
the born fetus shifts.

A fore- and future thought.
He exists at the edge of a harbor,
curled on a rock. Both leg and tail,
he is the rock that replaced the ship's deck
under pilgrims' feet, in the cold bay
or harbor of the mind, at the edge
of any ill-defined gulf

he leaves the land for water:
sinks. Fights his livid burka like a kitten
in a sack. The born fetus collects shed characteristics,
takes the meteorological view. Invited for remarks upon
this sweeping arm, this plume

2.

The born fetus lies in his crib.
Above him the op-art mobile swirls
like a complement of possible developments.
He stretches up a hand. The brain
nets and releases.

An almond's papery skin
imprints the fingertip

before the hand can reach—No almonds for baby!—
imprints on the throat. Throat tightens at the possible allergen,
subsides. Sigh. Almonds and olives in the next room,
cattle and cars in the next state, hands
of born fetuses across the globe at this moment:

He drags his hand through the air.
In the next room, navels roll from the table.
Delay—thud. Delay—countably.
Left gaping, the red plastic netting.

3.

A film parliament is convened in Rotterdam.
An attachment scrambles the interface; a fish parliament
convenes, a screen of swimming pixels, a string
of unrecognizable characters strong-arms the inbox. Cream

sinks and swirls in the stock. A thready pattern
collects, it is familiar. A hand rakes the air
with grapes and coefficients, from the rotting cupolas
and colonnades the godly leap
into firemen's nets and tarpaulins.
Grope for croutons. The charioteer
leans back, and with the tip of his whip
tickles the chin of the horse pursuant

4.

The born fetus is a born calculator.
Throat folds shut then—pop!—it opens.
On the plush

carpet of sensation, on the changing table,
the snug crux of the dilemma.
Are there always two or is it ten to the

With the blue foam cushion to hold him in the chair,
in the wash of the operating theatre,
in the lush cocktyllic suite,
the born fetus swirls among swirls.

He assembles indicia, stacks documents
inch-high, a citadel of one-storey
structures, over which he squats and flies
in a hand-built fantasy contraption.

5.

Light slots the seam in the curtain and picks out each part of the room.
It takes the day. On the monitor,
the red pulse makes the same gesture
over and over
as if waiting to be recognized.

The born fetus contemplates the fault tree.
The debris field of the mind
receives the sweep of a green arm.
It is a gentle, quiet gesture.
There are no people here and nothing can touch it.

Then electron-sized scapelettes
pivot and flash up a crown of brilliant sparks:
the doorlock reads the roomkey.

6.

The born fetus is held in arms
which provide no stop against propulsion.
In case of catastrophe,

he's as good as lost. Seeds pack the closed rinds
that pack the stands and think it over. Nth to the Nth.
Formula for miles above.
The born fetus is translated,

easily, from time to time. Slots through the lobe
of the sky. Over the looped track
where cars race, over rivers eating

caustic ribbons in the land:
deep familiar patterns
in the corpus

callosum
of the tennis courts;
in the red native lace
of Valencia, California.

Fence Books was launched in 2001 as an extension of *Fence,* a biannual journal of poetry, fiction, art and criticism that has a mission to redefine the terms of accessibility by publishing challenging writing distinguished by idiosyncrasy and intelligence rather than by allegiance with camps, schools, or cliques. It is part of our press's mission to support writers who might otherwise have difficulty being recognized because their work doesn't answer to either the mainstream or to recognizable modes of experimentation.

The Alberta Prize is an annual series administered by Fence Books in collaboration with the Alberta duPont Bonsal Foundation. The Alberta Prize offers publication of a first or second book of poems by a woman, as well as a five thousand dollar cash prize.

Our second prize series is the **Fence Modern Poets Series**. This contest is open to poets of either gender and at any stage in their career, and offers a one thousand dollar cash prize in addition to book publication.

For more information about either prize, visit our website at **www.fencebooks.com**, or send an SASE to: Fence Books/[Name of Prize], 303 East Eighth Street, #B1, New York, New York, 10009.

For more about *Fence,* visit **www.fencemag.com**.

Fence Books Titles

The Commandrine and Other Poems   Joyelle McSweeney

A Magic Book   Sasha Steensen
2004 ALBERTA PRIZE

MACULAR HOLE   Catherine Wagner

The Opening Question   Prageeta Sharma
2004 FENCE MODERN POETS SERIES

Sky Girl   Rosemary Griggs
2003 ALBERTA PRIZE

Nota   Martin Corless-Smith

APPREHEND   Elizabeth Robinson
2003 FENCE MODERN POETS SERIES

Father of Noise   Anthony McCann

The Real Moon of Poetry and Other Poems   Tina Brown Celona
2002 ALBERTA PRIZE

The Red Bird   Joyelle McSweeney
2002 FENCE MODERN POETS SERIES

Can You Relax in My House   Michael Earl Craig

ZIRCONIA   Chelsey Minnis
2001 ALBERTA PRIZE

MISS AMERICA   Catherine Wagner